Harbor of Refuge

MEDITATIONS BASED ON THE PSALMS

Jack Bateman

Harbor Of Refuge
Copyright © 1997 Jack Bateman

Published by WinePress Publishing
PO Box 1406
Mukilteo, WA 98275

Art created by Jack Bateman
Layout by **DENHAM**DESIGN, Everett, WA

All rights reserved. No part of this publication may be reproduced, stored in a retrieval system or transmitted in anyway by any means, electronic, mechanical, photocopy, recording or otherwise, without the prior permission of the publisher, except as provided by USA copyright law.

Printed on recycled paper in Canada
Library of Congress Catalog Card Number: 96-61944
ISBN 1-883893-95-X

This book
is dedicated to
my wife,
Marion

Jack Bateman

Thoughts from the Psalms to guide us along the way.

TABLE OF CONTENTS

Jack Bademan

Praise the Lord!

O give thanks to
the Lord for he
is good;
for his steadfast
love endures for ever!

PSALM 106:1

Patience is a quality we like to incorporate into our character. It is comforting when someone is patient with us when we are having difficulty grasping instructions or a new concept.

However, our own patience is severely tested along the path of our daily lives. In the world of business we may become impatient with a fellow worker who seems unable to understand the instructions we give. Repetition takes time—our time—and we resent it.

It happens in the classroom as teachers explain a rule or fact. A student is unable to comprehend it, so the explanation is repeated. Still, it is not understood. The teacher is tested; he can become angry or he can patiently approach the problem from another angle. Anger turns the student away. If the teacher regards him as a failure, the student comes to regard himself in the same light.

Parents need patience. What parent hasn't endured the "terrible twos"?

Physically tired from a day of work either at a job or at home, it is not easy to be patient with a child who is in opposition to our plans. The problem within the home is not confined to little children. As adolescents grow the yearning for independence increases and that frequently leads to problems that can be exasperating to parents and teenagers alike. It demands patience on all sides.

We marvel when we witness the patience of the Lord. How we must try His patience when we willfully insist on doing things our way! Yet the Lord never casts us aside and abandons us. Oh, we may be punished just as we may punish a naughty, stubborn child. But God's love is never lost just as we never stop loving our child no matter what he or she has done. A parent's love cannot be completely destroyed. Neither can the love of Almighty God. "His steadfast love endures forever!"

Put your hope
in God

God is our refuge and strength, a very present help in trouble. Therefore we will not fear though the earth should change, though the mountains shake in the heart of the sea, though its waters roar and foam, though the mountains tremble with its tumult.

Psalm 46: 1-3

Jack Bateman

PSALM 46:1-3

I love to stand on a beach and watch the waves curl and pound and explode in huge showers of spray. It is awesome during a Northeast storm. The power is overwhelming.

Years ago I was on a ship as it passed Gibraltar bound for New York on a stormy day in January. Waves towered over the ship as it rolled from side to side. At a time like that we need assurance. I want the presence of the Lord. It is comforting to know "God is our refuge and strength, a very present help in trouble."

Charts label the lighthouse at the entrance to Delaware Bay the Harbor of Refuge. The flashing light and bellowing horn is reassuring as each ship approaches, especially when the surging waves are threatening or when fog is so dense all other guides are lost. In times like that we find comfort in the words of the Psalmist: "Truly God is our refuge and strength."

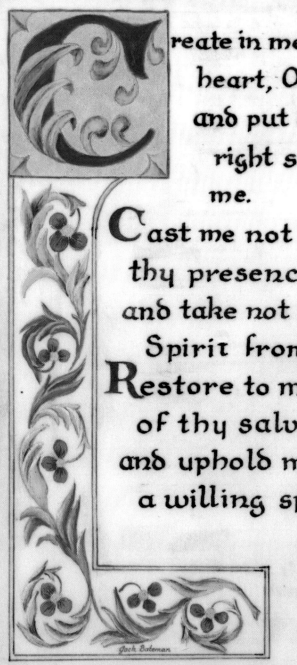

Create in me a clean
heart, O God,
and put a new and
right spirit within
me.
Cast me not away from
thy presence,
and take not thy Holy
Spirit from me.
Restore to me the joy
of thy salvation
and uphold me with
a willing spirit.

Psalm 51:10-12

Jack Bateman

PSALM 51:10-12

I think all of us desire a clean heart. By that I mean we want to be moral, law abiding citizens. We desire a clean conscience. With that we can face God and say, "I tried."

The trouble is we stumble here and there along the pathway of life. We say things we shouldn't, or we fail to say what we should have said. We do things we shouldn't or we fail to do what we should. Sometimes failing to do may be as serious as doing. A friend becomes hospitalized. We intend to visit him or her but put it off. Somehow we feel uncomfortable in that position; we don't know what to say or even how to act. We don't know how much the patient knows about his own condition and we're afraid we'll say something we shouldn't, or that we'll betray the seriousness of the case. So, we don't go, and we have a guilty conscience.

But when we pray about it and do whatever it was we didn't want to do, we feel better. God has "put a new and right spirit within us."

Now, there are some things we probably should not do. Unless we enjoy children it isn't advisable to serve as a teacher's aide. It requires patience to help in a nursing home.

Sharp words spoken in a flash of anger lead to regret and anxiety. A relationship with someone in the family or in the world of business or the church has been damaged. We pray about it and take steps to restore our relationship. The Psalmist pleads for God to create in us a clean heart and a new and right spirit within us. But success depends upon our willingness to come to the Lord with a contrite heart, a desire to submit our will to the will of God.

O Lord, truly
I am your servant

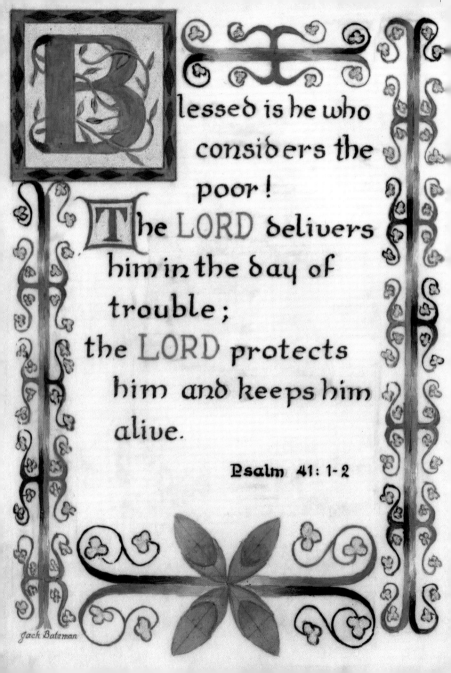

Blessed is he who considers the poor! The LORD delivers him in the day of trouble; the LORD protects him and keeps him alive.

Psalm 41: 1-2

Jack Batzman

PSALM 41:1-2

Most of us are plagued with what we term "junk mail." It consists of advertising things we don't want or need as well as appeals for contributions to an endless string of charities, many of them worthy. We wonder how we got on their mailing list. I suppose most people do what I do: select a few, support them as best I can, and discard the rest. It gives the conscience a bump because we want to help a just cause and sometimes we feel a little guilty throwing out those we reject.

In Mark 14:6 Jesus says, "You always have the poor among you and they badly need your help, and you can aid them whenever you want to."

We want to support cancer research and the in-roads medical science is making with MS. We want to combat AIDS. But there is a limit to what we can donate. So, we become selective as we support certain charities.

There are many wonderful people who donate time to serving in soup kitchens, providing meals for the homeless. There are others helping in clothing distribution centers. The giving of time is as significant as money.

There are other forms of poverty. Some people have a poor attitude. They are negative and oppose community projects designed to help less fortunate fellow citizens, especially if they see it as a threat to their wallets.

They are negative at their jobs. They put in time but are only interested in their paychecks. It's very difficult to deal with these people but they are here and we must try to help them if we can.

The Lord is my strength

and my shield

Make a joyful noise to the Lord, all the earth, break forth into joyous song and sing praises! Sing praises to the Lord with the lyre, with the lyre and the sound of melody! With trumpets and the sound of the horn make a joyful noise before the King, the Lord!

Psalm 98: 5-6

Jack Bateman

PSALM 98:5-6

How drab a worship service can be without music! Music touches our souls and dictates the moods we are in. Of course, we have different reactions to various kinds of music. Some respond to music described as rock. Others are caught up in opera and marvel at the unbelievable talent displayed. But there are plenty of people who emphatically state that they "can't stand opera." A great choir, such as the Westminister Choir or the Mormon Tabernacle Choir, can hold some people spellbound and move them to tears.

A church organ can create a range of moods depending upon the composition played. Trumpets, trombones, clarinets, strings and, of course, the human voice evoke an emotional response.

Music creates a mood. I recall a worship service I attended many years ago. A beautiful young woman sang and at the same time played her violin. It was professional in every respect and the spiritual quality was such that I still recall it. Music can do that.

There are some who will argue that it is the sermon, the verbal message that is important and we could dispense with music (and maybe the offering, too!), but music inspired by God is a part of worship. It helps in the development of a spiritual atmosphere.

Music was integrated into worship services centuries ago. The Old Testament recounts the use of instruments as a means of helping the congregation open their hearts as they worship the Lord. In Psalm 71:22 we read, "I will praise thee with the harp for thy faithfulness, O my God, I will sing praises to thee with the lyre, O Holy One of Israel." In Psalm 98:5-6 the Psalmist urges the worshiper to "break forth into joyous song and sing praises. Sing praises to the Lord with the lyre."

The Lord preserves the faithful

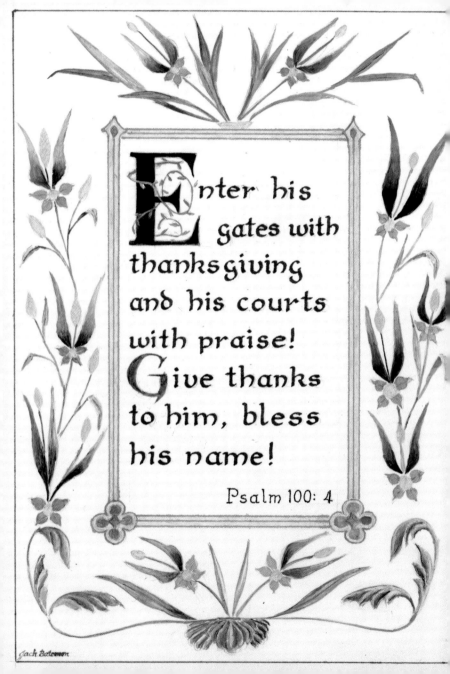

Enter his gates with thanksgiving and his courts with praise! Give thanks to him, bless his name!

Psalm 100: 4

PSALM 100:4

How much we take for granted! We approach the church, enter, sit in a pew and worship the Lord. We cannot imagine the church door locked. We assume the pastor or priest will be there as well as the choir and accompanist. Why shouldn't it be? That's our heritage.

But on the darker pages of history there have been churches that were closed. No one was allowed to enter. Preaching, singing hymns, and praying was forbidden.

We are fortunate. In the United States no matter what denomination or sect we choose to follow the doors are open. Moreover, in many churches the doors are open all week for a wide range of church-related or civic activities.

Let us enter His gates with thanksgiving. Give thanks to God for the blessings we enjoy. Let us be grateful for the freedom to worship.

We give
thanks
to thee
O God;
we give thanks.
We call on
thy name
and recount thy
wonderous ways.

Jach Bateman

Psalm 75:1

PSALM 75:1

In Luke 17:11-19 we are told of the ten lepers who approached Jesus and asked Him to have mercy on them. Jesus directed them to go and meet with the priests. On the way they were cleansed of a disease so terrible that its victims were ostracized. They were dependent upon scraps of food thrown to them or left for them. So dreaded were they that not even their shadow was permitted to cross the path of those whom they met.

Of the ten one, ". . . when he saw that he was healed turned back praising God with a loud voice, and he fell on his face at Jesus' feet giving him thanks. Now he was a Samaritan. Then said Jesus, 'Were not ten cleansed? Where are the nine?'"

How often do we receive a blessing and fail to give thanks? It may be a favor by a friend or family member. Perhaps a kind word received when we are depressed. Certainly, good health is a major blessing that we take for granted until we lose it.

Praise the LORD!
Praise the LORD, O my
soul!
I will praise the LORD
as long as I live;
I will sing praises to
my God while I have
being.

Psalm 146:1-2

Jack Bateman

PSALM 146:1-2

I suspect one of our chief vices is ego. There are areas in our lives where we succeed; in fact, in some things we excel. It may be in bowling or tennis or golf, or maybe in some specific task in an office or as an automobile mechanic. A dentist or a surgeon is admired for his skill.

We accept credit for that and begin to think we did it all by ourselves. But isn't it true that we succeed because of a combination of physical and mental qualities given to us by God? The success we enjoy can be attributed to our skill, our dedication, our work habits, but these are gifts from the Lord.

If we are given talent or skill we have a responsibility to use it to the best of our ability. But, we also need to give thanks to the Lord for our gift.

Psalm 68:19

Blessed be the Lord who daily bears us up; God is our salvation.

Jack Bateman

PSALM 68:19

There will always be a tomorrow. Though it may be overcast, the sun will rise each morning. Moreover, astronomers can pinpoint the exact moment the sun will appear. Science marvels at the precision and asks how it happens. Science always wants to know how things occur. And why.

A little girl races down the driveway, trips, falls, slides along the rough cement and scrapes her knees. She cries from the shock and pain. We pick her up, carry her into the house, wash her scraped knees, then carry her to a big chair where we hold her on our lap and cradle her. We want to pour out our love.

"Blessed be the Lord who daily bears us up." No matter how serious the fall, the Lord is there to support us. Truly, "God is our salvation."

Blessed is the man who makes the Lord his trust, who does not turn to the proud, to those who go astray after false gods.

Psalm 40:4

Jack Bateman

PSALM 40:4

It is clear the people of ancient Israel had trouble with their pride which led to inflated ego. And that led to ignoring the Lord and worshiping money, material possessions, status and much more. The Psalmist warned them that if they continued to worship these false gods it must follow that they no longer placed their trust in the Lord. In their ego they thought they could manage their affairs very well without God.

That sounds familiar, doesn't it? How many people today take undue pride in their achievements? No matter what the field, to become a leader requires skill, training and perseverance. We envy great achievers and emulate them, forgetting it is the Lord who gave them their ability to do so much.

It is well to listen to the Psalmist of ancient times. His words are just as pertinent today as the day they were written. Let us place our trust in the Lord.

The fear of the Lord is the beginning of wisdom; a good understanding have all those who practice it. His praise endures for ever.

Psalm 111: 10

Jack Bateman

PSALM 111:10

The Psalmist says, "The fear of the Lord is the beginning of wisdom." I prefer to substitute the word love for fear. It is the nature of love to be forgiving. Oh, yes, we can become angry with God for what we think is unfair treatment, but we still love him just as he, no doubt, becomes angry with us yet continues to love us.

In the multiplicity of our activities, as we seek to bring into reality our ambition, we tend to allow our ego to dominate our judgment. We forget that all we have is a gift from God.

To thank God for our talents is the beginning of wisdom. We should take time each day to express our love for the Lord. Those who recognize that their success is the result of hard work, plus talent granted by God, are wise indeed.

Blessed are those whose way is blameless, who walk in the way of the Lord! Blessed are those who keep his testimonies, who seek him with their whole heart, who also do no wrong but walks in his ways

Psalm 119:1-3

Jack Bateman

PSALM 119:1-3

Ships whose destination is Philadelphia must enter Delaware Bay where it flows into the Atlantic Ocean between Cape May on the north and Cape Henlopen to the south. The bay narrows and becomes the Delaware River. The 120-mile route is treacherous with rocky reefs and sand bars hidden beneath the surface. Buoys mark the channel, red on the right, green on the left. It is illegal for a ship to negotiate this stretch of water without a pilot based at Lewes at the mouth of the bay. It is the job of the pilot to be on the bridge to direct the watch at the wheel.

I find an analogy here. As we approach the Port there are buoys which are passages of Scripture and they serve as guides for us. Jesus, the Pilot, knows the course and leads us. It is our responsibility to heed His words and steer the course He tells us to follow.

"Blessed are those who walk in the way of the Lord," says the Psalmist. To walk with the Lord is an ideal which we strive to achieve. When we are receptive to the Pilot's instructions we shall arrive safely at the Port. Consider the words of the hymn "Jesus, Savior, Pilot Me" which concludes with the comforting words, "Fear not, I will pilot thee."

Let God be exalted!

Know that the Lord is God It is he that made us and we are his; we are his people and the sheep of his pasture.

Psalm 100:3

PSALM 100:3

We are told that sheep are gentle animals, quite defenseless when attacked by predators. This is not to say they have no minds of their own; they can be quite stubborn.

They depend on the shepherd to guide and protect them. They trust him completely; they know his voice and respond to it. A shepherd will attend them at their birth and will care for them if they become ill or injured.

The Psalmist likens us to sheep with the Lord as our shepherd. He guides us and protects us. We are His sheep and He loves us. How foolish we are when we resist his protective, loving care!

It is interesting to note that while there are those who reject the Good Shepherd, the Good Shepherd never rejects them. He is always willing to bring the wayward sheep into the fold. When we are hurt as we graze in the field of life the Shepherd cares for us. How fortunate we are to be the sheep of His pasture!

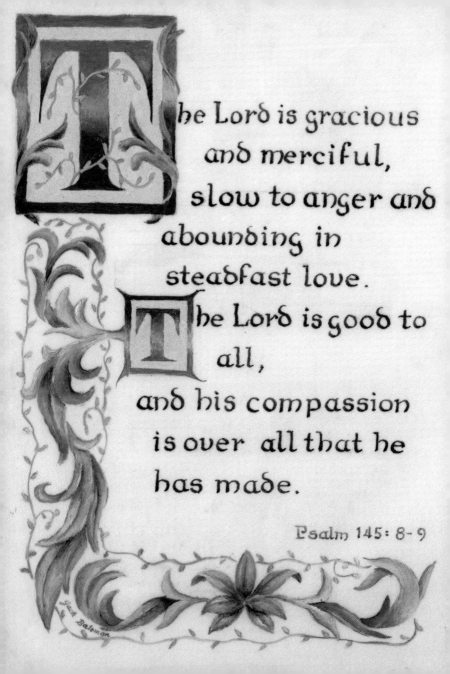

The Lord is gracious
and merciful,
slow to anger and
abounding in
steadfast love.
The Lord is good to
all,
and his compassion
is over all that he
has made.

Psalm 145: 8-9

PSALM 145:8-9

The Lord is gracious and merciful." These words by the Psalmist are comforting. Considering our failures and indifference, we marvel that the Lord is so merciful. Sometimes we are short-tempered; we snap at the people we love most. We don't mean to be disagreeable, but complications physical or psychological cause us to be cross. Parents, children, dear friends, the very people we love most of all are hurt. We are filled with remorse and we ask them to forgive us. And we make the same request of the Lord. That's when the Psalmist's words have their full meaning for us. How fortunate indeed that the Lord is gracious and merciful.

"The Lord is good to all," even those who break His commandments—which includes all of us. If we come to Him with a contrite heart we are told He is merciful, compassionate.

However, I believe we have a responsibility as we ask the Lord for His forgiveness. We are expected to incorporate that same love and mercy in our relationships with other people. That includes family members, business associates, and all the others whose path crosses ours occasionally. It takes in casual acquaintances as well as those whose work requires us to be together. We are expected to show the same compassion, the same reluctance to turn to anger. We need to remember the Psalmist's admonition.

God is our
an ever refuge
present and help strength, in
trouble

Trust in the Lord,
and do good;
so you will dwell
in the land, and
enjoy security Take delight in the
Lord,
and he will give you
the desires of your
heart.

Jack Bateman

Psalm 37: 3-4

PSALM 37:3-4

The barrier islands along the east coast from New Jersey to Florida have built sand dunes of varying heights. Subject to buffeting by the sea and wind, they are secured by thick grass. It grows in clumps and the roots are deep.

Developers, recognizing the desire for an unobstructed view of the ocean, have brought in bulldozers and leveled the dunes in preparation for building homes and condominiums. The result was predictable and disastrous. Storms push pounding waves across the beach and over the area once protected by the dunes. There is nothing to stop the swirling torrents of water, and few forces in nature are as powerful. Houses, standing like herons on their exposed pilings, have their plumbing dangling in a useless tangle.

So it is with our lives. Destructive forces surround us. Drugs, for example, will destroy us. Pride can interfere with our growth. Materialism can distort our values. Teaching based on the Bible forms the dunes in life. Church with its ritual, homilies, hymns, fellowship, classes and outreach is the grass that secures the dunes. The temptations we face are the developers that will destroy the dunes. If we give in and allow our dunes to be leveled we become vulnerable to every storm that comes along. Trust in the Lord and enjoy security.

Praise the Lord, O my soul

raise the Lord!

I will give thanks to the Lord with my whole heart,

in the company of the upright, in the congregation.

Psalm 111:1

Jack Bateman

PSALM 111:1

We have all heard someone say, "I don't have to go to church to worship God." I suppose there is some truth to that. Inspired by some beautiful aspect of nature or a magnificent musical composition we can find ourselves marveling at the source of the inspiration and give thanks to God.

But isn't that self-centered? There is a joy that comes with sharing our worship with others. The fellowship experienced in a congregation of worshipers cannot be equaled anywhere.

Moreover, we need to stand up and be counted. Those who condemn the church don't hesitate to state their feelings so that all may hear. It is important that we who love the Lord be equally vocal. All that we have is a gift from God. How can we fail to give thanks to the Lord by supporting a congregation?

And we, in turn, are supported by the congregation. In our darkest hours it is comforting to be surrounded by Christian brothers and sisters who are so supportive.

We need to stand firm in our faith and in all humility give thanks to Almighty God for our blessings. We need to be part of a group who stand unwavering in their worship of God. The Psalmist was so right when he said, "I will give thanks to the Lord with my whole heart and in the company of the upright, in the congregation."

Surely God
is our help

As for man, his days are
like grass;
he flourishes like a flower
of the field;
for the wind passes over it
and it is gone,
and its place knows it no more.
But the steadfast love of
the Lord is from everlasting
to everlasting
upon those who fear him,
and his righteousness to
children's children,
to those who keep his covenant
and remember to do his
commandments.

Jack Bateman

Psalm 103: 15-18

PSALM 103:15-18

Mankind passes through a succession of growth stages in a normal life span. It begins as an infant, then childhood, struggles through adolescence, enters adulthood, and finally tapers off with old age. It seems to confirm the Psalmist's observation that the successful man or woman "flourishes like a flower of the field."

But what is success? Some believe that to be truly successful they must hold positions of authority, perhaps in the field of politics, finance, industry or science. Others gain success in smaller more modest arenas.

It happens in small towns, suburban communities and sprawling cities. It includes dedicated teachers, nurses, doctors, firemen, policemen, social workers, clergymen. They exert a powerful influence on the little circle of society in which they work.

But if in time they pass away, as they inevitably must, there is comfort in the words of the Psalmist. He points out, "The steadfast love of the Lord is from everlasting to everlasting."

The Psalmist includes a conditional clause when he adds, ". . . to those who keep his covenant and remember to do his commandments."

So, if a life incorporates service to others and if we endeavor to remain faithful to the Lord and keep His commandments, the love of the Lord will always be with us.

It is good to

praise the Lord

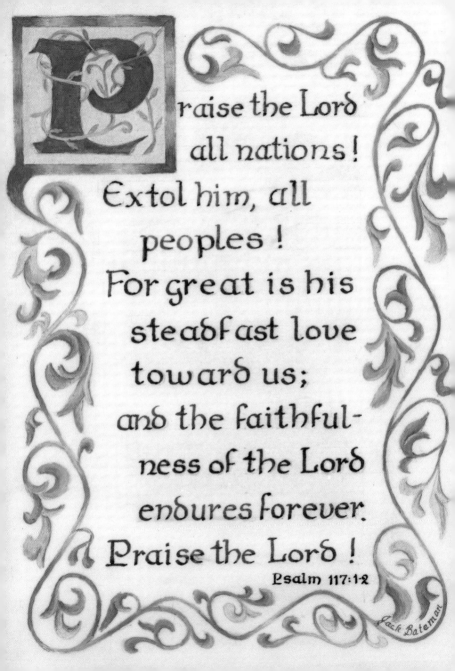

Praise the Lord all nations! Extol him, all peoples! For great is his steadfast love toward us; and the faithfulness of the Lord endures forever. Praise the Lord!

Psalm 117:1-2

Jack Bateman

PSALM 117:1-2

The rope that binds nations together is made up of many strands. There is the strand of economics—financial dealing. There is another of mutual military concerns. And of scientific research and educational exchanges. Also, ethnic ties. But the strands can become frayed and in time they may break. There is one that is vital and it is essential that it be protected and preserved. That strand is our united reverence for the Lord.

No matter that we may be divided over small issues within the fold of Christianity; Protestants and Catholics alike accept the basic precepts of their faith. God the Father is Lord over all. Jesus is the Christ, the Son of God. If we become divided on some issues we must stand shoulder to shoulder in praise of our Lord. And He will remain faithful to us—all of us. Thanks be to God.

The heavens are telling the glory of God, and the firmament proclaims his handiwork.

Psalm 19:1

Jack Bateman

PSALM 19:1

I have no understanding of astronomy, but I am impressed when I look up at night and see the star-studded sky. I recognize Orion and the Big Dipper, but that's the extent of my ability. I know that the stars are established in space and, weather permitting, we can locate them night after night. It is not by chance that this is so. God in His wisdom created it. The precision with which these heavenly bodies are placed is astonishing. That precision reflects the glory of its creator.

Whether in the heavens above us or on the earth around us, in the spectacular Grand Canyon or something as common as a maple leaf, the beauty of the creation is breathtaking. A brilliant sunset is awesome.

Can we ignore God in the presence of all this beauty? Can anyone shrug it off and say, "It just happened"?

Today's life forms have evolved from those that preceded them. All this development is the handiwork of God and we are richly blessed as we enjoy it.

In thee,
O Lord, do
I take
refuge.

Psalm 71:1

Jack Bateman

PSALM 71:1

Who among us has not experienced fear? Perhaps a physical threat, or maybe the dreaded possibility of the death of someone dear to us. At that moment we cry out to God to help us. The Lord not only becomes starkly real but also very personal. God is no longer a vague, abstract spirit we worship one hour a week in a church pew. God is the Creator, the Lord of all. He is all-powerful. We believe He can intervene for us, and in desperation we call out to Him. "Save my son!" "Save my wife!" "Lord, I'm drowning! Save me!"

"In thee, O Lord, do I take refuge." Why is it, I wonder, that we so often take God in stride putting Him on the shelf, so to speak, to be used in case of emergency? Then, when we're in trouble, when our car swerves off the road, we scream, "God save me!" Off the shelf. Very, very real. Very, very urgent.

Isn't it amazing how patient the Lord is? How sad it must make Him to have us approach Him only when we are in trouble.

Turn thou to me,
and be
gracious to
me;
for I am lonely
and afflicted,
Relieve the
troubles of my
heart,
and bring me out
of my distresses.

Psalm 25: 16-17

Jack Bateman

PSALM 25:16-17

Haven't all of us been overwhelmed with loneliness at some time in life? In the world of business to be in opposition to the unified thinking of colleagues is a very lonely feeling. To move to a new community separated from relatives and friends, not knowing anyone can create a feeling of loneliness.

Even in our churches where we join our close friends in worship we can be surrounded, yet feel depressed and lonely. The cause of our depression weighs us down. We cannot communicate our problem and they do not know that we carry such a heavy burden. It may be the critical illness of a relative, concern over a drug problem within the family, a teenage pregnancy in the family, a serious financial crisis. Whatever it is, we feel we cannot discuss it with anyone. And we become terribly lonely.

Then it is that we cry out to the Lord for help. That is when we can unburden ourselves and get the help we need. We realize we are not alone.

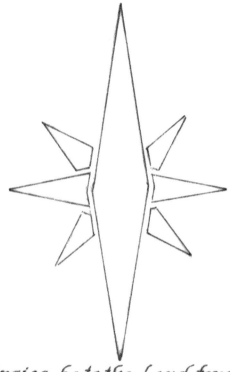

Praise be to the Lord forever!
Amen and Amen

To order additional copies of

Harbor of Refuge

please send $14.99*
plus $3.95 shipping and handling to:

Jack Bateman
4 Hoornkill Ave
Lewes, DE 19958

To order by phone,
have your credit card ready and call

1-800-917-BOOK

*Quantity Discounts are Available